AMERICA DEBATES ™

AMERICA DEBATES
PRIVACY VERSUS SECURITY

Jeri Freedman

rosen publishing's
rosen central®

New York

To my niece and nephew, Laura and Matthew Freedman, with love

Published in 2008 by The Rosen Publishing Group, Inc.
29 East 21st Street, New York, NY 10010

First Edition

Library of Congress Cataloging-in-Publication Data

Freedman, Jeri.
America debates privacy versus security/Jeri Freedman.—1st ed.
     p. cm.—(America debates)
Includes bibliographical references and index.
ISBN-13: 978-1-4042-1929-8 (library binding)
ISBN-10: 1-4042-1929-3 (library binding)
1. Privacy, right of—United States—Juvenile literature. 2. Civil rights—United States—Juvenile literature. 3. National security—United States—Juvenile literature. I. Title.
JC596.2.U5F74 2008
323.44'80973—dc22
                                                                                2007004749

Manufactured in the United States of America

On the cover: *(Left)*: A worker watches video surveillance monitors at the Department of Homeland Security Operations Center, Washington, D.C. *(Right)*: A demonstrator in Boston, Massachusetts, protests the Patriot Act and its effects on free speech.

CONTENTS

Introduction

On September 11, 2001, terrorists flew commercial airplanes into the twin towers of the World Trade Center in New York City and into the Pentagon, outside Washington, D.C. Three thousand people died, and the nation was stunned. It was the worst terrorist attack ever on American soil. The effect on America was galvanizing—all the more so because television brought the image of massive destruction directly into the homes of millions of Americans.

Most Americans thought they were safe from the violent terrorist attacks that afflicted countries in the Middle East and Europe. In the wake of the devastation of 9/11, they now felt vulnerable and scared. The events of 9/11 represented a new chapter in American history, the "Age of Terrorism." With this new reality came a new mind-set: "We are not as safe as we thought we were." It also brought with it a new determination to keep America and Americans free from terrorism. But at what cost? While no one wants to see another attack on America, we must also stop and think about what we are trying to protect. Part of the reason why America is a target of terrorists is because of what it represents: freedom of speech, freedom of religion, freedom to make money and seek a better way of life. These are freedoms that people all over the world yearn for— freedoms that threaten the control leaders have over the populations of some countries, especially in the Middle East.

This book examines the issues that arise in trying to balance the need to protect Americans against terrorist attacks with the need to preserve our most basic freedoms.

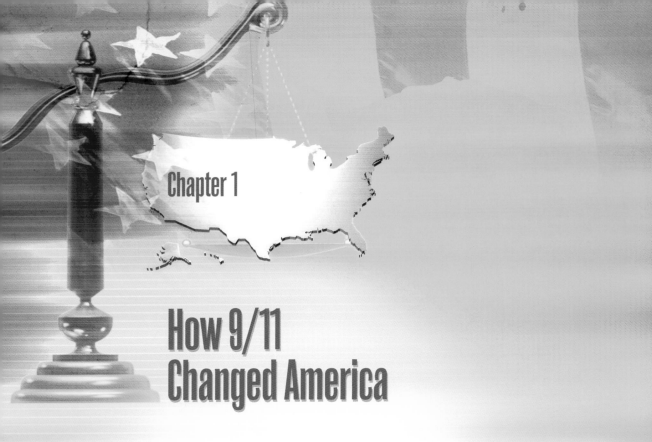

Chapter 1

How 9/11
Changed America

The attacks of 9/11 were not the first terrorist attacks on Americans in recent times. They were, however, the first in which foreign terrorists succeeded in killing Americans in the United States. Previous attacks were viewed by Americans as tragic incidents, but they were incidents that took place "somewhere else," much like the wars they sometimes saw on television. Now they realized the enemy could reach them right here at home.

THE DANGERS OF TERRORISM

Some effects of the events of 9/11 were immediate. Air travel dropped off, and across the country, half a million

This sign in Brooklyn, New York, was one of many memorials put up by Americans following the events of 9/11.

people in the travel industry lost their jobs. Traffic in other public places, such as malls and restaurants, dropped as well because people had heard of terrorist attacks on such places in other countries and thought they'd be attractive targets. Patriotism surged as people hung American flags outside their homes and businesses and vowed to defend America. The number of people enlisting in the U.S. armed services increased dramatically.

Other changes took place over the following months and years. They were more wide-sweeping and significant, and, some say, more harmful. The Department of Homeland Security was created by the president of the United States as a cabinet-level department. The powers of the Federal Bureau of Investigation (FBI) and Central Intelligence Agency (CIA) were expanded.

U.S. AGENCIES INVOLVED IN NATIONAL SECURITY

Department of Homeland Security: The agency responsible for the overall protection of America from terrorist attacks.

Central Intelligence Agency (CIA): The agency responsible for collecting and analyzing information about foreign governments, companies, and agents.

Department of Justice: The agency responsible for enforcing federal laws and prosecuting offenders who commit crimes against the United States.

Federal Bureau of Investigation (FBI): A branch of the Department of Justice, the FBI is the primary organization responsible for investigating crimes that violate federal laws.

National Security Agency (NSA): The agency responsible for monitoring, collecting, and analyzing foreign communications and intelligence information.

The Patriot Act was passed, giving national defense agencies vast powers of surveillance (monitoring) over citizens and the right to detain noncitizens without due process. These changes represent a departure from the previous view of America as a completely open society, where a citizen's activities and property are not to be interfered with or trespassed upon by the government. The events of 9/11 have caused many Americans to reconsider their values, to question whether absolute freedom is worth the risks it brings with it. The threat of terrorism has raised questions as to how much personal freedom Americans would be willing to give up for security, and whether giving up their freedom will indeed make them safe.

THE PATRIOT ACT

The Uniting and Strengthening America by Providing Appropriate Tools Required to Intercept and Obstruct Terrorism Act (USA PATRIOT Act) of 2001 was signed into law by President George W. Bush on October 26, 2001. It was reauthorized in 2006. This act, more commonly referred to simply as the Patriot Act, expanded the powers of federal law enforcement agencies, allowing them to better detect crimes against Americans, both at home and abroad. Changes were made to immigration and banking laws and to the powers granted to agencies involved in gathering intelligence information overseas. Many people felt that some changes were needed in existing laws to give law enforcement agencies a better ability to detect and stop terrorist acts before they were committed. But many people are also concerned that the powers granted under the

President George W. Bush signs the Patriot Act into law on October 26, 2001, giving the government new powers to monitor Americans' activities.

act could be misused. For example, the act created a new criminal category, "domestic terrorism." This is defined as engaging in activities in the United States that pose a danger to human life or violate the criminal laws of the United States or any state. It is also defined as trying to frighten or force members of the civilian population to perform an act against their will or to influence the government. As you can see, this provision is very broad and is vague enough to cover almost any crime.

The single biggest supporter of the Patriot Act is the U.S. government, which has declared that the expanded powers given to law enforcement agencies were necessary to detect potential terrorists and prevent them from committing terrorist acts. However, many people believe that provisions in the act violate the civil liberties of American citizens.

THE PATRIOT ACT AND CIVIL LIBERTIES

"Civil liberties" is a term used to describe the rights that protect a citizen of a country from unfair treatment by the government. Common civil liberties include the right for groups of people to assemble (get together), the right to free speech (including questioning or protesting government policies), and the right to freely practice one's religion. Many democratic countries have written down these rights in documents. In the United States, the Constitution describes a number of civil liberties that citizens have. These civil liberties are listed in the Bill of Rights, a series of amendments added to the U.S. Constitution before it was approved by the original thirteen states that formed America.

The Patriot Act will again be up for reauthorization in 2009. In the meantime, Americans have the opportunity to consider the pros and cons of the provisions in this act. We also need to think deeply about incorporating specific protections into the act to safeguard our liberties while still providing adequate tools to combat terrorists. We will explore the specific provisions of the Patriot Act, and the arguments for and against them, in more detail in the next chapter.

THE RIGHTS OF AMERICANS

The Bill of Rights consists of ten amendments to the U.S. Constitution that guarantee certain specific rights to American citizens. These amendments are:

Amendment I: Freedom of Religion, Speech, and Press

Congress shall make no law respecting an establishment of religion, or prohibiting the free exercise thereof; or abridging the freedom of speech, or of the press; or the right of the people peaceably to assemble, and to petition the Government for a redress of grievances.

Amendment II: Right to Keep and Bear Arms

A well-regulated militia, being necessary to the security of a free State, the right of the people to keep and bear arms, shall not be infringed.

Amendment III: Conditions for Quarters of Soldiers

No soldier shall, in time of peace be quartered in any house, without the consent of the owner, nor in time of war, but in a manner to be prescribed by law.

Amendment IV: Search and Seizure

The right of the people to be secure in their persons, houses, papers, and effects, against unreasonable searches and seizures, shall not be violated, and no warrants shall issue, but upon probable cause, supported by oath or affirmation, and particularly describing the place to be searched, and the persons or things to be seized.

Amendment V: Trial and Punishment

No person shall be held to answer for a capital, or otherwise infamous crime, unless on a presentment or indictment of a

As U.S. attorney general, Alberto Gonzales was responsible for defending the Patriot Act in cases where people claimed it violated their rights.

Grand Jury, except in cases arising in the land or naval forces, or in the militia, when in actual service in time of war or public danger; nor shall any person be subject for the same offense to be twice put in jeopardy of life or limb; nor shall be compelled in any criminal case to be a witness against himself, nor be deprived of life, liberty, or property, without due process of law; nor shall private property be taken for public use without just compensation.

Amendment VI: Right to a Speedy Trial, Confrontation of Witnesses

In all criminal prosecutions, the accused shall enjoy the right to a speedy and public trial, by an impartial jury of the State and district wherein the crime shall have been committed, which district shall have been previously ascertained by law, and to be informed of the nature and cause of the accusation; to be confronted with the witnesses against him; to have compulsory process for obtaining witnesses in his favor, and to have the assistance of counsel for his defense.

Amendment VII: Right to a Trial by Jury

In suits at common law, where the value in controversy shall exceed twenty dollars, the right of trial by jury shall be preserved, and no fact tried by a jury shall be otherwise reexamined in any court of the United States, than according to the rules of the common law.

Amendment VIII: Excessive Bail, Cruel Punishment

Excessive bail shall not be required, nor excessive fines imposed, nor cruel and unusual punishments inflicted.

Amendment IX: Construction of the Constitution

The enumeration in the Constitution, of certain rights, shall not be construed to deny or disparage others retained by the people.

Amendment X: Powers of the States and People

The powers not delegated to the United States by the Constitution, nor prohibited by it to the States, are reserved to the States respectively, or to the people.

Chapter 2

Surveillance of American Citizens

The Patriot Act contains sections called titles. Most of the issues that are controversial are found in Titles II and V. The following chapter looks at some of the activities that government law enforcement agencies are engaging in and presents the arguments for and against such activities.

PRE-9/11 SURVEILLANCE LAWS

The surveillance of Americans did not start with the events of 9/11. However, the limitations on what law enforcement could and could not do were much tougher prior to the Patriot Act. For example, before a federal law enforcement agent could wiretap a telephone or plant an electronic bugging device, that agent had to convince a judge that there was sufficient evidence to demonstrate that a crime had been or was about to be committed. The agent also had to specify exactly which phones would be tapped. Personal records such as those maintained by telephone companies could be obtained by a federal prosecutor only if they were relevant to a current criminal investigation. As will be discussed in the next few sections, the Patriot Act has reduced or removed many of these barriers to the monitoring of individuals' communications and personal records. Supporters of the act claim that this is necessary to find out about terrorists' activities before they carry out an attack. However, it has been shown in the past that widespread powers of surveillance can be abused.

PROVISIONS OF THE PATRIOT ACT

Title I: Enhancing Security Against Terrorism

This section sets up a fund for counterterrorism and allows the military to be called in to deal with threats from weapons of mass destruction. It charges the director of the Secret Service to develop a national network of electronic crime task forces to prevent, detect, and investigate electronic crime, including (but not limited to) potential terrorist attacks against electronic infrastructure (such as the Internet) and financial payment systems. It also authorizes the president to confiscate assets belonging to any "foreign person, foreign organization, or foreign country" that the president found had participated in an attack on the United States. In addition, if a suspect is charged based on classified information, the act allows the evidence to be reviewed secretly by a judicial authority without the presence or knowledge of the suspect and his/her attorney.

Title II: Enhanced Surveillance Procedures

This section significantly increases the powers of various federal law enforcement and intelligence-gathering agencies to engage in the surveillance of American citizens. The provisions of this section are discussed in more detail later in the text.

Title III: International Money Laundering Abatement and Anti-Terrorist Financing Act of 2001

This section expands the provisions for stopping money laundering. These provisions provide for increased communication between financial institutions and law enforcement agencies, including increased reporting requirements.

Title IV: Protecting the Border

This section increases the powers of investigation and enforcement of the Immigration and Naturalization Service and the federal attorney general.

Title V: Removing Obstacles to Investigating Terrorism

This section authorizes the collection and analysis of the DNA of people who are convicted of violent crimes. It enhances the sharing of information, obtained by electronic and physical searches, between foreign intelligence services such as the CIA and domestic law enforcement agencies such as the FBI. It also

The J. Edgar Hoover FBI Building in Washington, D.C., is the nerve center for the FBI's surveillance and antiterrorism activities.

requires companies to turn over the phone, financial, and educational records of customers when presented with the proper documentation, called National Security Letters, and to keep such requests secret from the customer being investigated.

Title VI: Providing for Victims of Terrorism, Public Safety Officers, and Their Families

This section sets up aid to victims of terrorism and those who are killed in the line of duty because of terrorist acts.

Title VII: Increased Information Sharing for Critical Infrastructure Protection

This section allows federal agencies to fund and contract with local and state organizations to fight terrorism.

Title VIII: Strengthening the Criminal Laws Against Terrorism

This section sets out the penalties for committing different types of terrorist acts.

Title IX: Improved Intelligence

This section describes how the CIA should go about sharing foreign intelligence information so that it is used effectively.

Title X: Miscellaneous

This section deals with a variety of specific issues not dealt with elsewhere in the act.

TERRORIST OR CRIMINAL?

The Foreign Intelligence Surveillance Act (FISA) was passed in 1978 because people feared that foreign agents might engage in terrorist acts against U.S. targets. However, there was evidence at the time that the FBI had engaged in illegal surveillance of nonterrorists such as civil rights leader Dr. Martin Luther King Jr. and Vietnam War protesters. These were people who challenged the beliefs and political positions of those in power and were exercising their First Amendment rights of free speech. Because of such actions by government agents, the public and lawmakers viewed it as necessary to limit the power of government agencies to engage in activities such as wiretapping. Congress decided that it would be allowed to use such powers only against people suspected of being potential terrorists or spies, and not against people suspected of being engaged in ordinary crimes.

SURVEILLANCE

The Patriot Act has expanded the range of surveillance activities that federal law enforcement agents can engage in with less burden of proving a legitimate reason for doing so. It gives federal agents the ability to monitor e-mail, perform sneak-and-peak searches, and monitor phone and Internet usage. It also allows them greater access to library and bookstore customer records and personal credit, financial, medical, and educational information. Supporters of the act claim that this type of surveillance is necessary to find evidence that a person is engaged in terrorist activity. Individuals and organizations concerned about the rights of Americans fear that the scope of powers granted to authorities under this act allows the government to monitor the records and activities of all Americans. This, they say, violates their privacy and civil rights guaranteed under the Constitution. The following sections look at some of the specific activities authorized under the act and the positions of various parties concerned with these activities.

The U.S. Justice Department has demanded that Internet search services turn over their records, exposing the private information of millions of users.

Monitoring of Phone and E-Mail Activity

Title II of the USA Patriot Act allows federal law enforcement agencies to use electronic devices to monitor electronic communications, such as those over telephones and the Internet. The act also allows federal agents access to Internet-related information such as records of e-mail addresses, "to" and "from" names, and the addresses of Web sites users visit. The orders for surveillance must be approved by one of eleven federal district court judges. Those who have had their rights violated by having their communications intercepted have the right to sue those who undertook the surveillance. However, since the law forbids companies turning over the records from telling customers about the surveillance, people may not even know they are being surveilled until they are accused of wrongdoing.

The powers granted are not supposed to be used in violation of the First Amendment rights of American citizens. (In other words, they are not supposed to be used to interfere with the right to free speech.) However, opponents of the law believe that people will be intimidated from exercising their right to free speech if they know that anything they say could be misinterpreted and used against them.

Sneak-and-Peak Searches

The Patriot Act also gives federal law enforcement authorities the right to conduct what are commonly called sneak-and-peak searches. Law enforcement officials can enter a person's home, search through that person's belongings, read and photograph letters and documents, and read and copy files on the computer. The authorities can do this secretly without that person ever knowing that they were there.

Monitoring Bookstore Purchases and Financial, Medical, and Educational Records

In normal criminal investigations, law enforcement agents cannot obtain access to a person's medical or financial records without demonstrating that the records are relevant to an ongoing investigation. In addition, they must obtain a court order from a judge or a subpoena from a grand jury. The person whose records are sought also has the right to challenge this access in court. The Patriot Act, however, allows agents to insist that such records be turned over immediately, without notifying the person being investigated, with the result that the person has no chance to object. This approach has raised a great deal of controversy, not just from citizens who don't want their records scrutinized but also from companies being asked to provide the records. This was the case when agents began using the act to obtain records from bookstores and libraries so they could see what books people were reading. Some libraries began purging circulation records more frequently to protect their users. When the federal government began demanding phone activity records from telephone companies, a number of companies refused to turn the records over.

ARGUMENTS IN FAVOR OF ALLOWING INCREASED SURVEILLANCE—CATCHING TERRORISTS BEFORE THEY ACT

The most significant argument in favor of the Patriot Act and the expansion of the powers of surveillance is that such surveillance is necessary to catch potential terrorists before they can pull off a significant act of terrorism. This is especially true of provisions that allow for roving surveillance, to track potential terrorists who keep switching cell phones for instance. In the past, phone taps were limited to specific phones, rather than being issued for all phones used by a person. Provisions such as these can be seen as simply adjusting the law to encompass technologies that did not exist at the time that earlier laws were written. The act also allows organizations whose jurisdiction is domestic crime, such as the FBI, and

A policeman escorts a worker injured in the first terrorist attack on the World Trade Center, in 1993. The FBI began expanding its powers of surveillance following that attack.

those whose area of responsibility is international, such as the CIA, to share information with each other. Most people, regardless of where they stand on other provisions of the act, feel that this type of interagency cooperation is beneficial.

More controversial is the U.S. government's claim that the overall expansion of the powers of surveillance granted to government law enforcement agencies is justified solely because it is the most efficient process for uncovering terrorist plots before they can be carried out. For example, the U.S. Department of Justice issued a report in July 2004 called "Report from the Field: The USA Patriot Act at Work," which states, "The USA PATRIOT Act equips federal law enforcement and intelligence officials with the tools they need to mount an effective, coordinated campaign against our nation's terrorist enemies. The Act revised counterproductive legal restraints that impaired law enforcement's ability to gather, analyze, and share critical terrorism-related intelligence information."

Agencies such as the FBI no longer have to present convincing evidence to a grand jury to obtain a warrant to engage in certain types of surveillance. However, agents must still convince a judge that the information they seek to obtain is relevant to a legitimate terrorist or criminal investigation, and not just the pursuit of people exercising their legitimate right to free speech—for example, by protesting government policies they disagree with.

ARGUMENTS AGAINST ALLOWING INCREASED SURVEILLANCE— PROTECTING OUR CIVIL LIBERTIES

Those opposed to the Patriot Act note that there is nothing in the act that would keep the government from engaging in widespread spying on Americans in general. The head of the FBI claims that the agency will carry out its duties in a responsible manner, but that doesn't mean that, now or in the future, another head of such an agency won't misuse the increased powers of surveillance. For example, in a July 2003 report, "UNPATRIOTIC ACT: The FBI's Power to Rifle Through Your Records and Personal Belongings Without Telling You," the American Civil Liberties Union, an organization dedicated to protecting the rights of Americans, states, "The USA PATRIOT Act vastly expands the FBI's authority to monitor people living in the United States. These powers can be used not only against terrorists and spies but also against ordinary law abiding people. . . . Indeed, the FBI can use these powers to spy on any United States citizen or resident."

While, realistically, it seems unlikely that the government would spy on ordinary citizens for no reason, there are two gray areas that are worrisome. The first is the case of individuals who represent a threat or inconvenience to those in authority. For instance, ecological protesters often publicize practices by large corporations that are bad for the environment. If those running such a corporation, or major stockholders or board members, are friends of those in power, could the protesters be placed under surveillance in order to find any reason to prosecute them? The second area of concern is people of ethnic origins similar to those of the terrorists who represent the most likely threat to the United States—such as Arab or Asian Muslim immigrants. Are these people as a whole likely to be the subjects of surveillance, just because of their ethnic background? How does this affect those who are totally law abiding or those who are not immigrants, but merely have Asian or Arab ancestry?

Reduced Protections

There are two major aspects of the Patriot Act that are worrisome: (1) its provisions apply not just to people suspected of terrorism, and (2) it reduces the requirements for law enforcement and intelligence-gathering organizations to demonstrate a legitimate reason for engaging in such surveillance of an individual. The first issue means that such surveillance can be applied to people suspected of committing ordinary crimes, removing many of

Under the provisions of the Patriot Act, members of activist groups like Greenpeace may come under increased government surveillance.

the protections provided by the normal legal process. The second issue not only can potentially inhibit individual liberty but may also lead to innocent people being wrongly accused or having their lives disrupted.

In other words, when law enforcement personnel must show that there is strong evidence that a person is involved in a crime in order to obtain a search warrant or wiretapping order from a judge, there is a greater chance that there really is strong evidence against that person.

The Patriot Act also blurs the distinction between terrorist and nonterrorist crimes. For example, many of the provisions in the act apply to those engaged in terrorism or any "violent crime," and the new category of "domestic terrorism" includes any "violent crime." This makes it possible to engage in surveillance of anyone involved in just about any major crime, and some minor crimes.

Why should we care if people engaged in nonterrorist crimes are surveilled? After all, they're criminals. Or are they? One reason for this important distinction is that some protesters deliberately or accidentally engage in illegal, nonterrorist acts in the process of, for instance, antiwar or pro-ecological demonstrations. These acts include trespassing, disturbing the peace, vandalism, and defacing government property. Therefore, authorities could easily justify tapping the phone of anyone engaging in protesting any policy about anything, on the basis that they might commit a crime.

Furthermore, this provision goes against constitutional protections that require a person who commits a crime to be considered innocent until proven guilty. Capturing terrorists may justify extraordinary measures. However, when dealing with ordinary criminals, there is no justification for abandoning all the constitutional and legal protections designed to protect the innocent.

Chapter 3

Profiling

Profiling is a tool used by law enforcement agencies to narrow down the field of suspects who may have committed or plan to commit a crime. Like other tools, it can be used properly, or it can be misused.

WHAT IS PROFILING?

Offender profiling, or psychological profiling, is a tool used by law enforcement authorities to identify a person who has committed or is likely to commit a crime. Authorities draw up a collection of characteristics that are typical of people who commit a particular type of crime. When that type of crime is committed, they then use that profile to help identify the person most likely to have done it. Profiles are commonly used, for instance, to track down serial killers.

In contrast to offender profiling, racial profiling is based primarily on the race or ethnic origin of the person being profiled. In the wake of the 9/11 attacks, many people became suspicious of any person who was of Middle Eastern origin, or at least any Middle Eastern male, since the terrorists were all men. In an attempt to combat terrorism, many men who looked as if they might be Middle Eastern or Asian Muslims were subjected to special searches at airports and sometimes denied passage on airplanes.

ARGUMENTS IN SUPPORT OF PROFILING

The following are some of the arguments in support of profiling:

1. The men who have carried out attacks against the United States in the past have been Middle Eastern or Asian Muslims with radical beliefs. Therefore, it is possible that future acts will be carried out by the same type of person, especially if suicide attacks are involved, because engaging in that type of attack requires a certain fanaticism. Given the number of terrorists arrested in the United States and abroad, there is some justification for believing that terrorists are likely to fit this mold.

2. What many detractors refer to as racial profiling is, in fact, legitimate offender profiling. For example, there was a great deal of outcry in 2006 when several

This airport surveillance photo shows Mohammed Atta and Abdulaziz Alomari, two of the Arab Muslim hijackers involved in the September 11, 2001, attacks on the World Trade Center.

respected Muslim clerics were removed from the gate of an airport where they were waiting to board a plane. The men were detained as possible terrorists on the basis of "suspicious" behavior. Opponents of racial profiling claimed the clerics had simply been praying in Arabic and cited their detention as an example of the abuse of racial profiling. Officials involved in the detention claimed, however, that the men were not detained simply because they were dressed like Muslim clerics or had been speaking Arabic. They claimed that a number of passengers had overheard the men talking and referring to Osama bin Laden (head of the Al Qaeda terrorist organization), and one man had requested a seat belt extender (a long strap with a large buckle on one end) when he obviously didn't need one. (This was one of the signs of suspicious behavior that airline staff had been told to look for because the extender could be used as a weapon.) Was this a case of a lot of small bits of erroneous, but legitimate, evidence piling up, or a case where the men were targeted primarily because they were Arab Muslims?

ARGUMENTS AGAINST PROFILING

The following are some of the arguments against profiling:

1. The fact that many terrorists are Muslim men does not mean that any significant number of Muslim, Arab, or Asian men are terrorists. This is logic at its simplest: because a cat is an animal, it does not follow that all animals are cats. The majority of men who fit the physical profile will be law abiding, and many will be American citizens whose constitutional rights are violated by search and possible detention without any cause to be suspicious of them in particular.

Imam Omar Shahin (*opposite page*) was one of six Muslims barred from boarding a flight in Minneapolis, Minnesota, in 2006. Authorities cited "suspicious behavior" as the reason for detaining him. Shahin said he and the others were merely praying.

2. Terrorists could be one step ahead of authorities. If it becomes widely known that security agencies in the United States are focusing only on dark-complexioned men, terrorists will start using women or Anglo men to carry out their dirty work. And, once again, American law enforcement, busy concentrating on "locking the barn door after the horse has escaped," will be caught off guard.

3. Relying on overly simple approaches to finding terrorists leads to lazy, sloppy analysis of potential dangers. Authorities look for people who fit their preconceived notions of possible terrorists, rather than looking for any evidence of suspicious activity. For example, while authorities are busy pulling Indian businessmen out of airport security lines for scrutiny because they look like "Middle Eastern terrorists," some disaffected white American teenager gets through with the ingredients for a dangerous weapon.

DO SECURITY PROVISIONS UNFAIRLY TARGET MINORITY AND IMMIGRANT COMMUNITIES?

There is increased fear that foreign nationals may sneak into the United States, or enter legally but stay beyond the time allowed by their visas, in order to engage in terrorism. This has led to the targeting of immigrant communities as possible sources of terrorists. There have been unjustified attacks on legal immigrants, and even American-born citizens of Middle

After 9/11, the Immigration and Naturalization Service began a special registration program for men from mostly Arab and Muslim countries. These women took to the streets of New York to protest the program.

Eastern and Asian ancestry. In some cases, these people have been surveilled, denied passage on airplanes, and detained.

This fear has also led to a national movement to find and deport immigrants who are in this country illegally. Supporters of this approach claim that deporting illegal immigrants will make America safer by ensuring that all immigrants are documented. They further claim that it's unfair to immigrants who enter the country legally if those who entered illegally are allowed to stay. Those who oppose the anti-illegal-immigrant movement point out that most of the terrorists who engaged in the attacks of 9/11 entered the country through legal channels. So, simply weeding out illegal immigrants will not address the problems of dangerous foreign nationals being in the country. Indeed, terrorist organizations are well funded and capable of creating false documentation that will allow their members to enter the country legally. In addition, the largest group of illegal aliens in the United States come from Mexico, and no one has discovered a hotbed of Mexican terrorists. Some of those who feel that immigrants are being unfairly targeted believe that the anti-immigrant efforts are aimed at keeping America white and Anglo, rather than at catching terrorists. A case can be made that the entire anti-immigrant efforts take up time and money that could better be spent looking for specific terrorists in a more focused fashion.

Chapter 4

The Right to Privacy

There is no place in the Constitution where the right to privacy is explicitly stated. Most people who believe that we have the right to privacy point to the amendments in the Bill of Rights, such as the Fourth Amendment, which prohibits unreasonable search and seizure. The right to privacy encompasses two main areas, which are discussed in the following sections.

THE RIGHT TO GO ABOUT OUR BUSINESS WITHOUT INTERFERENCE

The right to go about our business without interference means that we are free to engage in our daily activities,

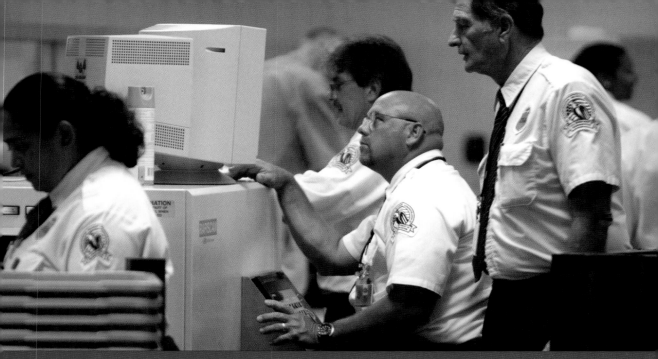

Transportation Security Administration screeners check passengers boarding flights across the United States. Keeping potential terrorists from boarding planes is a constant concern.

such as working, reading, traveling, and the like, without the government restricting such activities. Most people are prepared to put up with a reasonable amount of inspection in the course of their daily activities because they feel that it makes them safer. We expect to show ID when using a credit card or cashing a check because it protects us against someone else stealing our money. And although no one likes to stand in security lines at the airport, we feel safer knowing that someone has checked the baggage going onto the plane for weapons or bombs. Such behavior does not restrict our ability to travel. In contrast, measures such as "no-fly" lists, which were implemented by the government in the wake of the 9/11 terrorist attacks, do infringe on individuals' right to move freely. A no-fly list is a list of suspected terrorists that airlines check prior to allowing passengers to board the plane. If a person's name appears on this list, then that person is not allowed to fly.

Sounds like a good idea not to let terrorists fly, doesn't it? The two problems with this list are that (1) many people have names that are the same as, or similar to, those that appear on the list, and these people are wrongly prevented from flying, and (2) this is the type of system that creates a false sense of security. It can make the public feel better about flying because people think that they are being protected, when it's quite easy for a real terrorist to get false papers and travel under an assumed name, while innocent travelers' movements are being restricted.

THE RIGHT NOT TO HAVE OUR PERSONAL INFORMATION USED AGAINST US

As stated by Bruce Schneier in a *Wired News* article, "The Eternal Value of Privacy," one of the most common arguments used by those who feel that the right to privacy is not an issue when implementing security measures is, "If you have nothing to hide, why do you care?" The most relevant response to this question comes not from a modern-day organization such as the American Civil Liberties Union, but, as Schneier points out, from Cardinal Richelieu, the chief minister to King Louis XIII of France in the seventeenth century. Richelieu said, "If one would give me six lines written by the hand of the most honest man, I would find something in them to have him hanged."

GOVERNMENT SURVEILLANCE IN U.S. HISTORY

There have been a number of times in U.S. history when the government felt that the danger from foreign influences warranted the passage of special laws or programs to combat those forces. The following are some of these:

The Sedition Act of 1918: This act was passed during World War I specifically to outlaw antigovernment criticism while the country was at war. It was not repealed until 1921.

COINTELPRO (Counterintelligence Programs), 1956–1971: These were a series of programs carried out by the FBI to keep tabs on a wide range of groups that the government claimed were engaged in subversive activities. Surveillance was carried out against such groups as the Weathermen, a radical group that advocated the violent overthrow of the U.S. government during the 1960s and 1970s. However, it was also used against organizations such as Dr. Martin Luther King Jr.'s nonviolent civil rights group, the Southern Christian Leadership Congress.

The Foreign Intelligence Surveillance Act (FISA) of 1978: This law laid out the regulations for engaging in the surveillance and search of persons suspected in engaging in international terrorism or espionage for a foreign power. In contrast to the Patriot Act, it required convincing proof that a suspect was engaged in such activities in order to obtain a warrant for searches and surveillance.

The Antiterrorism and Effective Death Penalty Act of 1996 (AEDPA): Passed in the wake of the bombing of the Alfred P. Murrah Federal Building in Oklahoma City in 1995, this act expanded the government's power to investigate and prosecute those engaged in terrorism. Many of its provisions relating to terrorism, access to citizens' personal records, immigration, and other areas were expanded in the Patriot Act.

One of the most basic issues in the right to privacy debate is the right not to have our personal information used against us. The Privacy Act of 1974 prohibits the government from compiling secret databases on American citizens. One reason for this is that it protects groups of citizens who belong to a given race, ethnic group, or religious or political persuasion from being singled out by the government. Yet, despite the Privacy Act, such massive data gathering is being carried out today. An article, "America Wrestles with Privacy vs. Security," by Brad Knickerbocker, appeared in the July 22, 2005, issue of the *Christian Science Monitor*. It reported, "The FBI has been gathering thousands of pages of intelligence on such organizations as the American Civil Liberties Union (ACLU) and the environmental group Greenpeace. Other groups that have been

Noel Saleh and Michael Steinberg of the ACLU and Nazih Hassan of the Council on Islamic-American Relations talk about their lawsuit against the U.S. government's secret surveillance program.

part of peaceful protests find that they are being investigated as well."

The Department of Justice claims that there have been no proven incidents of any American's civil liberties being violated. However, contrary to this claim, numerous lawsuits have been brought against the government by people who have been prevented from boarding planes at airports, detained erroneously, or required to secretly turn over their customers' records to the government. In addition, since in most cases those complying with surveillance orders are forbidden to reveal this fact, people's rights may indeed have been violated without their knowledge.

THE PSYCHOLOGY OF FEAR

The issue of privacy is about more than protecting ourselves. It's about being able to go about our business without the fear that something we say or do will be misunderstood and get us in trouble with government watchdog agencies. The very fact that the debate over privacy versus security is raging indicates that many people have such fears. This type of fear affects our quality of life and restricts our freedom far more than searches at the airport.

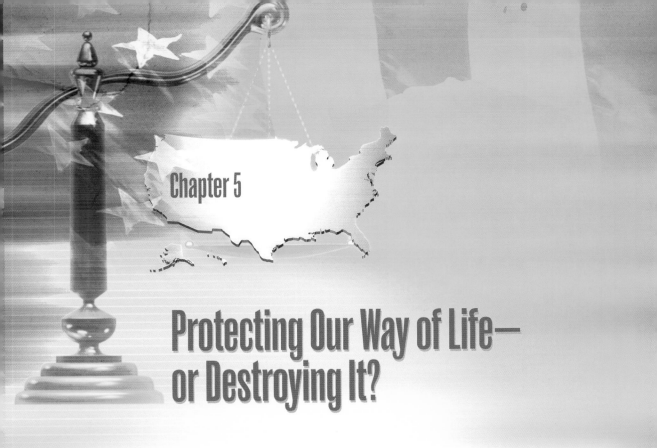

Chapter 5

Protecting Our Way of Life— or Destroying It?

Many of the arguments over the expansion of government powers of surveillance are related to the rights guaranteed to Americans by the Constitution. The following sections explore these issues.

IS THE PATRIOT ACT UNCONSTITUTIONAL?

Questions about the constitutionality of the Patriot Act usually arise primarily in relation to three amendments in the Bill of Rights: the First Amendment, the Fourth Amendment, and the Fifth Amendment. The First Amendment guarantees Americans the right of free speech. However, the exercise of free speech can be inhibited in ways other than passing laws that forbid people to, for example, criticize the government. If people are afraid to speak freely, then this, too, interferes with the right of free speech.

The Fourth Amendment protects American citizens from unreasonable searches and the seizure of their property, including documents, by requiring that sworn evidence be provided of wrongdoing. This amendment was included in the Bill of Rights by the founders of the United States because they had experienced firsthand having their homes and businesses searched repeatedly by British soldiers looking for evidence of revolutionary activities. The Fifth Amendment states that American citizens will not be subject to prosecution without due process of law being followed, including the right to challenge their accusers.

Legitimate Power or Reduction of Rights?

Those in favor of the Patriot Act claim that it merely expands upon powers granted to law enforcement agencies in previous acts and laws. They claim that such expansions of power are necessary to adequately track down terrorists. They point to the fact that the government has been granted special powers before when dealing with foreign agents who represent a threat to America's security.

Those who wish to control powers granted under the Patriot Act claim that when earlier laws, such as the Foreign Intelligence Surveillance Act (FISA), gave the government special powers to surveil foreign agents, those powers were limited to cases in which there was evidence that certain people were foreign agents. FISA laws also contained specific provisions to protect

American civilians against the misuse of such powers. In contrast, some of the provisions in the Patriot Act forbid the owners of businesses to tell customers that their records are being searched or to discuss the search. These new rules can also inhibit the right to free speech and deny both the owner of the business and the owner of the records the right to challenge the government's right to search their property in court.

The Voice of the People

The public's concern with these issues is widespread. In fact, more than 400 communities around the United States have passed resolutions supporting the reforming of the Patriot Act to include checks and balances to protect citizens' constitutional rights. Organizations supporting efforts to regulate the powers granted under the Patriot Act range from liberal organizations like the American Civil Liberties Union to conservative organizations like the American Conservative Union.

This illustrates an important point. In the end, the critical element in protecting civil liberties is not what's written explicitly on a piece of paper. It's what we, as 300 million Americans, are willing to accept. The strongest tool to keep the government in check is the voice of the people. Several times in recent years, the public as a whole has objected so strongly to activities undertaken by the government that the authorities have been forced to rein in those activities. This power works regardless of which side of the debate one is on. Both when the government wanted to give control of security at major U.S. ports to a company based in an Arab country and when it wanted to establish a special court in Guantánamo Bay, Cuba, to try

An activist shows signatures of people who oppose the Patriot Act. Americans have the right to use such petitions to tell government leaders how they feel about issues.

detainees in secret, objections by the U.S. public were so great that the government was forced to alter its plans. By voting and/or e-mailing, faxing, or calling their representatives in the House of Representatives and Senate, the people themselves, acting together, can be their own best defenders.

IS WHAT WE ARE GAINING WORTH THE COST?

In the wake of the attacks of September 11, 2001, the primary concern of a vast number of Americans became protecting themselves against terrorism. But the question is, at what cost? Polls have shown that the majority of Americans fully expect that someday there will be another terrorist attack on the United States. Most Americans want to see that law enforcement agencies are given adequate tools to keep the chances of a terrorist

WORDS OF WISDOM

The debate over privacy versus security did not start in the twenty-first century. The following are some comments made by lawmakers of previous eras:

"Those who would give up Essential Liberty to purchase a little Temporary Safety, deserve neither Liberty nor Safety."
—*Benjamin Franklin, American statesman (1706–1790)*

"The true danger is when liberty is nibbled away, for expedience, and by parts."
—*Edmund Burke, British statesman (1729–1797)*

"Experience should teach us to be most on our guard to protect liberty when the Government's purposes are beneficent. Men born to freedom are naturally alert to repel invasion of their liberty by evil-minded rulers. The greatest dangers to liberty lurk in insidious encroachment by men of zeal, well-meaning but without understanding."
—*Louis Brandeis, Supreme Court justice (1856–1941)*

"The framers of the Constitution knew human nature as well as we do. They too had lived in dangerous days; they too knew the suffocating influence of orthodoxy and standardized thought. They weighed the compulsions for

restrained speech and thought against the abuses of liberty. They chose liberty."
—*William O. Douglas, Supreme Court justice (1898–1980)*

"There is little value in insuring the survival of our nation if our traditions do not survive with it. And there is very grave danger that an announced need for increased security will be seized upon by those anxious to expand its meaning to the very limits of official censorship and concealment."
—*John F. Kennedy (1917–1963), 35th president of the United States*

act to a minimum. For example, terrorist acts are usually complicated and require a lot of coordination among the people involved. Much of this activity is carried out over electronic media such as the Internet and cell phones. Therefore, agencies such as the National Security Agency claim, with some justification, that monitoring network traffic can help to identify active terrorist cells before they can engage in a major act of terrorism. It should be noted, however, that this type of monitoring only looks for patterns in electronic transmissions, such as repeated calls to numbers suspected to be connected to terrorist

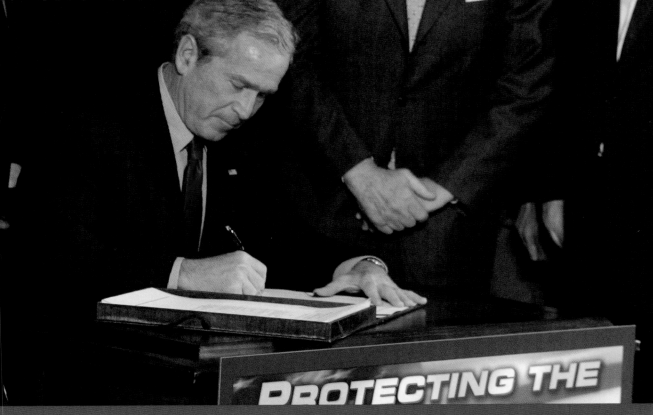

PROTECTING THE

In a scene that mirrors the original signing of the Patriot Act, President George W. Bush signs the bill reauthorizing the Patriot Act on March 9, 2006.

activities. It does not refer to the monitoring of the content of phone calls.

Those who wish to see adequate controls placed on the use of surveillance point out that there is no evidence that having adequate checks and balances on the usage of such tools keeps them from being used where there is legitimate need for them. In other words, they are asking, "If there is reason to believe that a person is a terrorist, why can't you produce some evidence that supports that?" Or, perhaps more important, "If you don't intend to violate anyone's civil liberties, why do you object to including in the legislation specific rules that limit this possibility?"

While it would certainly be more convenient for government law enforcement agencies if they could surveil all the activities of all Americans any time and any way they wanted, this would not necessarily make us safer. It would, however, most likely result in the constant fear that what we did and said might be misinterpreted and used against us. If we give up the very liberties that so inflame the terrorists, then the terrorists will have won without firing another shot.

WHERE DO WE GO FROM HERE?

Clearly, we need to both protect ourselves from terrorists' attacks and safeguard our rights and freedoms. Therefore, one could argue that the real debate is not whether to do one of these things or the other. Rather, it is about how to best go about doing both these things at the same time. This, obviously, requires making some trade-offs. The authorities may not have as free a hand to do anything they wish without any checks and balances. Those deeply committed to personal freedoms may have to accept more inconvenience in their lives, as long as there are adequate protections to guarantee that such intrusions are truly justified. The real question is: how much latitude do those on each side of the debate get, and how do we guarantee that they do not overstep their bounds or interfere with the legitimate needs of the other side?

Timeline

1978   The Foreign Intelligence Surveillance Act is passed, expanding the government's power to deal with foreign agents.

February 26, 1993 Four terrorists set off a car bomb under the World Trade Center in New York, killing 6 and injuring 100.

April 19, 1995 Timothy McVeigh sets off a car bomb in front of a federal building in Oklahoma City, killing 168 and injuring 600.

1996   The Antiterrorism and Effective Death Penalty Act is passed; it contains many provisions later incorporated into the Patriot Act.

July 1996 A bomb set off at a concert during the Olympic Games in Atlanta, Georgia, kills 2 and injures 110.

August 1998 Terrorist bombings of U.S. embassies in Nairobi, Kenya, and Dar es Salaam, Tanzania, leave 263 dead and 5,000 injured.

October 2000 Terrorists bomb the USS *Cole* in the Yemeni port of Aden, killing 17.

September 11, 2001 Terrorists attack the World Trade Center in New York and the Pentagon in Arlington, Virginia.

September 26, 2001 The USA PATRIOT Act is signed into law.

October 20, 2001 President George W. Bush creates the Office of Homeland Security.

2002 A military prison camp is established at the U.S. naval base in Guantánamo Bay, Cuba, to house foreign nationals suspected of being involved in terrorism. The treatment of prisoners there raises concern in the United States and abroad.

November 25, 2002 The Homeland Security Act of 2002 makes the Department of Homeland Security a cabinet-level agency of the U.S. government.

January 29, 2003 The American Library Association issues a resolution stating its belief that certain sections of the Patriot Act violate the constitutional and privacy rights of library patrons.

January 23, 2004 The U.S. Supreme Court makes its first ruling against a provision in the Patriot Act when it rules in favor of the Humanitarian Law Project, stating that classifying "giving expert advice or assistance" as terrorism violates the First and Fifth Amendments.

September 30, 2004 The U.S. Supreme Court rules in favor of the ACLU, declaring that the requirement in the Patriot Act that Internet service providers turn over records to the FBI on presentation of National Security Letters, which don't require a court order, is unconstitutional.

April 6, 2005 Senators Larry Craig (R-ID), John Sununu (R-NH), and Richard Durbin (D-IL) propose the Security and Freedom Enhancement Act, which would place safeguards on the powers granted by the Patriot Act.

January 1, 2006 The U.S. government agrees to pay $200,000 to settle a lawsuit brought by the ACLU over the "no-fly" list.

March 9, 2006 The Patriot Act is reauthorized for another three years.

June 19, 2006 The U.S. Supreme Court declares that prisoners held in Guantánamo Bay are protected by the Geneva Conventions, an international set of rules that govern how prisoners of war must be treated.

2009 The Patriot Act is scheduled for reauthorization.

Glossary

beneficent Intended to do good.

Bill of Rights Ten amendments added to the U.S. Constitution that spell out rights guaranteed to Americans.

civil liberties The rights that protect citizens from unfair treatment by their government.

compensation Payment.

compulsion A hard-to-resist urge.

Constitution The document drafted by the founding fathers of the United States and approved by the original thirteen states that explains the principles by which the United States shall be governed.

counterterrorism Efforts to stop terrorist acts.

detractor One who feels and speaks negatively about something.

due process The applying of the law in such a way that a person is not denied his or her rights and in line with basic accepted legal principles.

encroachment Trespassing on another's area or property.

expedience Convenience.

grand jury A special jury that reviews evidence to see if there is enough to indicate that a crime has been or is being committed, as opposed to a regular court that determines the guilt or innocence of a person.

Guantánamo Bay A location on the southeast coast of Cuba where the U.S. government has a naval base where people suspected of being or aiding terrorists are detained and questioned.

insidious Harmful in a sneaky way.

intelligence Information gathered and analyzed to find clues to significant activity.

jurisdiction Area of responsibility.

legislation Laws proposed or passed by Congress.

legitimate Legal or in line with accepted principles.

money laundering The process of taking money from or being destined for an illegal source and passing it through a legitimate business to make it look as if the money is from a legitimate source.

offender profiling A law enforcement tool in which the characteristics of known offenders are used to judge how likely a suspect is to be responsible for a crime.

redress To right a wrong.

subpoena A document issued by a judge that requires someone to provide physical evidence or appear as a witness in court.

surveillance Watching and monitoring the activities of someone.

trespass To enter the property of another person without his or her permission.

warrant A legal document that allows the searching of a location or the arresting of a person.

For More Information

American Civil Liberties Union
125 Broad Street, 18th Floor
New York, NY 10004
Web site: http://www.aclu.org

Amnesty International
5 Penn Plaza, 14th Floor
New York, NY 10001
(212) 807-8400
Web site: http://www.amnestyusa.org

Central Intelligence Agency
Office of Public Affairs
Washington, DC 20505
(703) 482-0623
Web site: http://www.cia.gov

Electronic Privacy Information Center
1718 Connecticut Avenue NW, Suite 200
Washington, DC 20009
(202) 483-1140
Web site: http://www.epic.org

Federal Bureau of Investigation
J. Edgar Hoover Building
935 Pennsylvania Avenue NW
Washington, DC 20535-0001
Web site: http://www.fbi.gov

U.S. Department of Justice
950 Pennsylvania Avenue NW
Washington, DC 20530-0001
(202) 514-2000
Web site: http://www.usdoj.gov

U.S. Department of State
2201 C Street NW
Washington, DC 20520
(202) 647-4000
Web site: http://usinfo.state.gov/is/international_security/
    terrorism.html

WEB SITES

Due to the changing nature of Internet links, Rosen Publishing
has developed an online list of Web sites related to the subject
of this book. This site is updated regularly. Please use this link
to access the list:

http://www.rosenlinks.com/ad/adps

For Further Reading

Bridegam, Martha. *The Right to Privacy*. New York, NY: Chelsea House, 2003.

Frank, Mitch. *Understanding September 11: Answering Questions About the Attack on America*. New York, NY: Viking, 2002.

Fridell, Ron. *Privacy vs. Security: Your Rights in Conflict*. Berkeley Heights, NJ: Enslow Publishers, 2004.

Friedman, Laurie S. *Introducing Issues with Opposing Viewpoints: Terrorism*. Chicago, IL: Greenhaven Press, 2005.

Hudson, David L., Jr. *Open Government: An American Tradition Faces National Security, Privacy, and Other Challenges*. New York, NY: Chelsea House, 2005.

Kallen, Stuart A. *Are Privacy Rights Being Violated?* Chicago, IL: Greenhaven Press, 2004.

McGwire, Scarlett, and Paul Dowsdell. *Surveillance: The Impact on Our Lives*. Chicago, IL: Raintree, 2001.

Nakaya, Andrea C. *Current Controversies: Homeland Security*. Chicago, IL: Greenhaven Press, 2004.

New York Times. *A Nation Challenged*. New York, NY: Scholastic Reference, 2002.

Ojeda, Auriana. *Civil Liberties*. Chicago, IL: Greenhaven Press, 2004.

Bibliography

American Bar Association. "The Patriot Debates: A Sourceblog for the USA Patriot Debate." Retrieved December 13, 2006 (http://www.patriotdebates.com).

American Civil Liberties Union. "National Security: The Patriot Act." Retrieved December 3, 2006 (http://www.acluprocon.org/bin/procon/procon.cgi?database=5%2dJ%2dSubs%2edb&command=viewone&id=4&op=t).

Darmer, M. Katherine B., Robert M. Baird, and Stuart E. Rosenbaum. *Civil Liberties vs. National Security in a Post-9/11 World*. Amherst, NY: Prometheus Books, 2004.

Knickerbocker, Brad. "America Wrestles with Privacy vs. Security." *Christian Science Monitor*, July 22, 2005.

Leone, Richard C., and Greg Anrig Jr., eds. *The War on Our Freedoms: Civil Liberties in an Age of Terrorism*. Cambridge, MA: Perseus Books, 2003.

Posner, Richard A. *Not a Suicide Pact: The Constitution in a Time of Emergency*. New York, NY: Oxford University Press, 2006.

Schneier, Bruce. "The Eternal Value of Privacy." Wired News. May 18, 2006. Retrieved December 22, 2006 (http://www.wired.com/new/columns/0,70886-0.html).

Simplytaty.com. "Timeline of Terrorism." Retrieved December 24, 2006 (http://www.simplytaty.com/broadenpages/terrorism.htm).

U.S. Department of Justice. "Preserving Life and Liberty." Retrieved December 13, 2006 (http://www.lifeandliberty.gov).

Bibliography

Yoo, John C., and David Cole. "Is the Patriot Act Unconstitutional?" MSN Encarta. Retrieved December 23, 2006
(http://encarta.msn.com/sidebar_701713501/Is_the_Patriot_
Act_Unconstitutional.html).

Index

Index

ABOUT THE AUTHOR

Jeri Freedman has a B.A. from Harvard University. She is the author of a number of other nonfiction books published by Rosen Publishing, including *Primary Sources in American History: Colonies—Massachusetts* and *America Debates Civil Liberties and Terrorism*. Under the name Ellen Foxxe, she is the coauthor of two alternate history science fiction novels. She lives in Boston.

PHOTO CREDITS